Christian Crackers
Church Chuckles

Collected by

PHIL MASON

MONARCH
BOOKS

Editorial office:
Monarch Books, Broadway House, The Broadway, Crowborough, East Sussex TN6 1HQ

British Library Cataloguing Data
A catalogue record for this book is available from the British Library.

Cartoons by Mike Buecheler

DESIGNED AND PRODUCED FOR THE PUBLISHERS BY
GAZELLE CREATIVE PRODUCTIONS
CONCORDE HOUSE, GRENVILLE PLACE, MILL HILL, LONDON NW7 3SA.
PRINTED IN SINGAPORE.

Notice in the kitchen of a church hall:

"Ladies: when you have emptied the teapot please stand upside down in the sink."
To which has now been added:
"No hot bottoms on the formica."

Outside a Canadian Baptist Church:

Church parking only
Violators will be baptised

**Seen outside a Birmingham Church
on November 18th:**

Come this Sunday and avoid the Christmas rush.

Notice outside a North London Church:

Wanted – workers for God.
Plenty of overtime.

Vicar, from pulpit:

"I would be grateful if the member of the congregation who keeps calling out, 'Praise the Lord!' would kindly cease and remember that this is the House of God."

From Wales:

A lady was collecting the Christian Aid envelopes. Calling at one house she met the response, "Sorry, I can't give you anything, the dog ate the envelope."

"Ah," responded the collector, "Don't worry, I have a spare envelope."

Back came the quick reply, "It's no good, he'd only eat that one too."

"Drink," said the Irish preacher, "is the curse of the country. It makes ye quarrel with yor neighbors, it makes ye shoot at yor Landlord, and it makes ye miss him."

Jane was quite a character. It appeared that she never washed or changed her clothes except from summer to winter, and vice versa, so the "perfume" heralded her arrival.

One Sunday morning after the service I noticed that her hands were filthy, so I remonstrated with her. This did not rile her at all. She merely replied quite serenely, "Well, you see, sister, it's like this. I usually makes me pastry on a Saturday but I couldn't yesterday. That's why me hands are dirty today."

From the mission field:

The Sacristan was so pleased to inform the congregation that their priest had recovered from his illness, he displayed the following notice:

God is good
The Vicar is better

A lady was very nervous about her appointment with the dentist. Before leaving home she sought courage by reading the text for the day from her calendar. It was Psalm 81 verse 10:

"Open thy mouth wide and I will fill it."

On the Sunday after Christmas at St. Mark's Church, Hamilton Terrace, London the lights failed just as Evensong was about to commence. Undaunted the curate and congregation found one or two candles and in the almost complete darkness of this large church proceeded with the service.

Meanwhile (unknown to the others) the Youth Club leader, an electrician by trade, had gone down to the Crypt to check fuses.

At the opening sentence of the third collect, "Lighten our darkness, we beseech thee, O Lord," the lights came on again.

The story goes that some delegates to a church conference in Scotland set off between sessions to explore the countryside. Presently they came to a stream spanned by a rickety bridge and started to cross, ignoring the warning to keep off.

A local inhabitant ran after them

in protest. Misunderstanding his concern, one of the visitors called, "It's alright, we are Anglicans from the Conference."

"I'm no' caring about that," was the reply, "but if ye dinna get off the bridge ye'll all be Baptists."

Seen on a church notice board:

When you were born, your mother
brought you here.
When you were married, your
partner brought you here.
When you die your friends will
bring you here.
Why not try coming on your own
sometimes?

Two Sunday fishermen heard bells
ringing in the distance. One said contritely:
"You know, Sam, we really
ought to be in church."
Sam rebaited his hook and thought for a
moment. "Well, I couldn't go
anyway, the wife is sick."

The church members were meeting to discuss raising money to repair the roof. A wealthy member stood up and said he would donate £5. As he sat down a bit of ceiling fell on his head. He rose again and said he would make it £50. Another member was heard to say, "Hit him again, Lord."

Bishop David Sheppard, former England cricketer, shares the following true story about his wife Grace, who is a governor of a comprehensive school. On one occasion when the governors were interviewing for the appointment of Deputy Head the chairman of the governors introduced her with the words: "This is Mrs Bishop, the wife of the famous footballer."

A Cranford housewife was talking to an American visitor about the difficulty in getting domestic help. She added how lucky she was to have a daily help.

"My," said the American, "Is that something religious?"

Sign outside small Kent church:

"Come early and get a back seat."

**A notice outside Chichester Cathedral
advertising lunchtime concerts read:**

"Sandwiches may be eaten."
Someone had scrawled underneath:
*"So if you are a sandwich
don't come."*

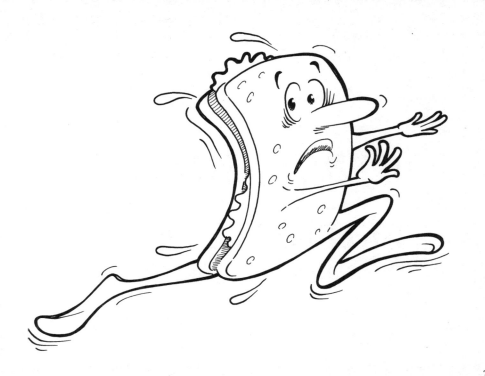

Notice outside a church in Warwickshire:

"Pray, do not park here."

A new Christian wrote to the Inland Revenue:

"I can't sleep at night so I am enclosing £100 I forgot to declare.

"P.S. If I still can't sleep I will send the rest."

A Baptist minister complaining about traffic noise in Harpenden is reported as saying, "Sometimes when we have something on in church all hell is let loose."

Definition of a committee:

A committee is a collection of the unfit
chosen from amongst the unwilling
by the incompetent to do the unnecessary.

Man in pub, to War Cry seller:
"Do you save young girls? Well,
save one for me."

Open All Hours

A Somerset man and his wife visiting Canterbury Cathedral were approached by an American tourist who asked: "Say – is this place open on Sundays?"

From Suffolk:

A farmer was reading the lesson at a
morning service. As he reached the bottom
of the page he read the words
"and Moses was sick." He then turned over
two pages at once, and continued,
"and the lot fell on Aaron."

From Wales:

In Swansea there is a well known firm of solicitors, W.G. Christian and Sons. A letter was sent to them from overseas, addressed simply: W.G. Christian, South Wales.

It eventually arrived at their office with a note from the Post Office attached which read:

"No Christians in Cardiff – try Swansea."

Two American tourists were staying in a small village in the heart of rural England. Come Sunday they attended the village church. The service was long, uninspiring, and the music rather dull. After the service the vicar greeted his two visitors and offered to show them around the church. As he pointed out various items of interest they came to a plaque on the wall with a list of names on it. "Whose are all these names?"asked one of the visitors, "Oh, those are the names of our parishioners who have died in the services," explained the Vicar. "And how do you intend to make it safe for those who are here now?" asked the other visitor.

Wrong List

Visiting another priest, a cleric offered to assist by hearing confessions. Since he was rather deaf and people tend to whisper in the confessional, parishioners were asked to write their sins on a piece of paper and pass them over.

This worked quite well until one woman handed him a slip bearing a message: "1/2lb tea, 1/2lb butter, 2lb sugar, 1/2lb cheese." The woman could only reflect bitterly on the list of sins she had left with her grocer.

"We are pleased to note that there has been a change of mind by the Housing Department regarding a name for the new housing complex for the elderly. 'St Peter's Close' did seem inappropriate."

You – Me – And Us

An old lady who was often the total
congregation of a tiny West Country church
was asked how they managed.
"Oh, we're fine," was her confident reply.
"Vicar does the 'God be'ses', and I do the
'As it wases.'"

Dr Robert Runcie recalls:

I remember encountering a lady in one of the parishes where I was bishop who had taken the scriptural phrase, "Drink ye all of this" to mean that when it came to her turn to take the chalice she drained it completely.

At a small Northamptonshire village in the 1920s the lady of the manor was churchwarden and treasurer, and used to order the communion wine by the case which was stored in her cellar until required. One Sunday morning we were ready to begin Sung Eucharist when the rector discovered he was out of wine. A choirboy was despatched to the Hall with instructions to ask the maid for a bottle of communion wine. In the meantime the service began, and when the boy returned, the bottle was hastily taken into the vestry, poured into the cruet and the service went on. Afterwards, the churchwarden came into the vestry and said: "Rector, may I see the bottle of wine you are using?" He duly produced it. "Just as I thought," she said, "It's beer!"

After Christmas three children were asked what they had done on Christmas Day. One, the son of the Vicar, said that the family had been to church, then arriving home had opened their presents and sung a carol. A Roman Catholic boy said he had been to Mass, then opened his presents and later sung carols. A little Jewish boy said that his father owned a toy factory, and after breakfast they had visited the factory, looked at the empty shelves and sung "What a friend we have in Jesus."

A lady describing the small attendance at her church said: "When the Vicar says 'Dearly Beloved', I blush."

A bishop, a boy scout and the Brain of Britain were passengers in a small aeroplane. The pilot announced serious trouble and asked everyone to leave the plane. There were only two parachutes so the bishop suggested that as he was the oldest he should stay behind. The scout said:

"Don't worry, sir, there are still two parachutes – the Brain of Britain has jumped with my haversack."

Half time

Until recent years many village nonconformist chapels were heated by a large coke stove situated in the middle of the room. One shrewd chapel steward, during the singing of the hymn before the sermon, used to put a whistling kettle on the stove. One week the visiting preacher commented afterwards that that was a sure way of timing the sermon! "Ah, yes sir," he replied, "but with some of the preachers us gets 'ere, I only half fills the kettle."

An old Cockney lady who attended Mission services regularly could not be persuaded to receive the sacrament, always protesting that she wasn't good enough. Finally convinced that there wasn't a qualification she knelt at the rail and on receiving the wine raised the glass heavenward and said: "Your very good 'ealth."

The minister was visiting an elderly lady and agreed to pray with her that she might have better health. They knelt together on the floor and he began: "Dear Lord, if it be your will, restore Mrs McIlroy to her former health." He felt someone touch him on the arm. "Excuse me," said the old lady, "Call me Lizzie, he won't know me by my married name."

Our church speakers sometimes pick up the local taxi messages. Recently, just as the minister said "Amen" at the end of the prayers, the message boomed out through the speakers: "Request understood and will be dealt with promptly."

**A notice outside an evangelical church
advertised the first two talks
in their autumn series**

First Sunday:
Jesus walks on the water

Second Sunday:
Searching for Jesus

Queen Victoria was out one Sunday with her faithful servant John Brown. She noticed someone fishing from a boat on the Loch. "Fancy people doing that on the Sabbath," she remarked. "But Ma'am, the Lord Jesus was in a boat on the Sabbath." The Queen turned and replied sharply, "Two wrongs don't make a right."

From the Parish News

We are delighted to report that the choir raised £120 for the building fund during their recent sponsored sing. This included £10 not to do it again.

Definition of a good sermon:

"It should have a good beginning and a good ending – as close together as possible."

A Benedictine monk was returning from a conference abroad and as customary packed his monk's habit in a small case. When he arrived at the customs the officer asked him: "Anything to declare?" The monk replied: "Only an old Benedictine habit." "O.K.," said the officer, "How many bottles?"

Definition of a committee:

"A committee is a dark avenue down which good ideas are lured and quietly strangled."

A bus stop was sited close to the church which had a wayside pulpit notice board on which was boldly painted: "Where will you be on judgement day?"
Underneath someone had written: "Still waiting for a number 125 bus."

Comment from a parishioner in the diocese:

"Our vicar's sermons always have
a happy ending.
The moment they've ended
everyone feels happy."

A nun driving her jeep in the Middle East ran out of petrol. The only container she could find was a chamber pot, in which she collected petrol and with great difficulty refilled the jeep. Some Arabs looking on observed, "Sister, we don't share your religion, but we admire your faith."

From America:

Readers of Centre View, a local newspaper in the Northern Virginia suburbs of Washington D.C., were startled by this headline:

HOLY SPIRIT NOW OFFICIAL LUTHERAN.

The story went on to discuss the organisation of a new congregation, Holy Spirit Lutheran Church, Centreville, Va.

SPOONERISMS

The original spoonerism, we are credibly informed, took place when the Rev. Archibald William Spooner, conducting worship in the chapel of New College, Oxford, announced the first line of a hymn as

"Kingquering congs their titles take."

His subsequent verbal bloomers delighted hundreds of Oxford undergraduates who obviously added to the range. He became famous for telling an absent youth,

"You have hissed my mystery lesson."

During a wedding service he is reputed to have told the groom:

"It is kistomary to cuss the bride."

At a Harvest Festival service it was announced,

"Gifts would be sent to the nick and seedy."

One day when visiting the Dean of Christchurch Dr Spooner asked the Dean's secretary:

"Is the bean dizzy?"

On another occasion when a visitor
remarked how beautiful the church looked
he enthusiastically replied,

"Many thinkle peep so."

And speaking about Queen Victoria he referred to her as

"Our Queer Dean."

A lady deacon was preaching at a small village church in North Yorkshire. She was welcomed by the churchwarden, a lady. The organist was also a lady, and there were eight ladies in the congregation. The first hymn was sung with great gusto, "Stand up, stand up for Jesus," especially the verse that runs, "Ye that are men now serve him, against unnumbered foes. Your courage rise with danger, and strength to strength oppose." Sadly it seemed their courage had failed them, for there was not one to be seen!

An Irish bishop tells how some people get nervous when they have to call him "My Lord". On one occasion as a lady was serving him a cup of tea she picked up the sugar bowl and said,

"How many Lords, my lump?"

At the end of his sermon the minister told his congregation that Jesus had called him to another church. The congregation then sang lustily "What a friend we have in Jesus."

I am a Reader, and during an interregnum my name and address was amongst those to contact for Church Information. Answering a knock at the door I was confronted by two little girls aged about seven and nine years with a baby in a pram. They asked: "Mummy says can you christen our baby?" My first reaction was to ask them if they had brought their own water.

While addressing the crowd at Speaker's Corner in Hyde Park, the distinguished Methodist Minister Lord Soper was interrupted by a heckler who kept shouting: "What about flying saucers?" Finally Lord Soper turned to him and, much to the delight of his audience, silenced him with: "I cannot deal with your domestic difficulties now."

An elder of the Wee Free's on the west coast of Scotland visited an old lady. She asked him if he would like a glass of lemonade.

He replied:

"It is not an occasion for lemonade."

"Would you like a glass of home made wine?"

"It is not an occasion for wine."

"Well, would you like a glass of whisky and water?"

"It is not an occasion for water."

From the USA:

An American schoolmistress returned from a visit to England and was telling her pupils of some of the wonderful sights she had seen. She referred to Lincoln Cathedral.

"Is there a Lincoln Cathedral in England?" asked one of the girls.

"Certainly there is and it is one of the most beautiful of all," was the reply.

"Say!" exclaimed the girl, "Wasn't it just sweet of them to name it after him?"

An American's observation of Heaven and Hell:

Heaven is where the police are British, the chefs are French, the mechanics German, the lovers Italian and the whole thing organised by the Swiss.
Hell is where the chefs are British, the mechanics French, the lovers Swiss, the police German, and it is all organised by the Italians.

At a Theological College it was the custom to vary the canticles and psalms from day to day. Announcing the Te Deum one morning the Principal, who was rather absent minded, began cheerfully: "We Praise Thee, O God," then added hastily, "Oh no we don't – it's Friday."

From Scotland:

Many of the young people who came to our youth club were real rough diamonds. It wasn't long before the fruit of our ministry began to take effect – the wheel hubs were stolen from our car. As time passed some of the tearaway teenagers started to take an interest. The result of this was an obvious improvement in their lives. Obviously struck by remorse two of the young lads approached me, and admitted stealing the hub caps. To their credit they produced replacements for the stolen goods. I thanked them and asked how they had managed to afford the replacements.

"Oh, that was easy," came the response. "We stole them from a guy's car who lives round the corner from us."

Two nuns out shopping had difficulty in parking their car. One suggested, "I'll drive around and pick you up later." The other completed her shopping and then looked up and down the street, finally asking a man, "Have you seen a nun in a red mini?" "Not since I went on the wagon," was the man's reply.

Only on Sundays (from Canada):

'Morbus Sabbaticus' is a peculiar disease:
1. The symptoms vary but never interfere with the appetite
2. It never lasts more than 24 hours
3. No doctor is ever called
4. It is contagious

The attack comes on suddenly on Sunday mornings. The patient wakes as usual, feeling fine, and eats a hearty breakfast.

Then, at about 9 a.m., the attack strikes and lasts until noon; then the patient is much improved and is able to take a ride, visit friends, watch TV, work in the garden, play golf, mow the lawn, or read the Sunday papers. He is then able to eat a full supper, but the attack often comes on again and lasts through the early evening. The patient is able to go to work on Monday as usual.

This ailment is often fatal to the soul.

A young missionary served in a remote part of Africa with few resources. But he did manage to convert some of the natives. One day, unarmed, he was walking through the bush when he was confronted by a lion.

He knelt in prayer, hands clasped, and after a few moments opened one eye and saw that the lion was kneeling down and had his paws clasped.

"My goodness," he said in relief, "are you a Christian too?"

"Yes, certainly," the lion replied, "I was just saying grace."

Seen on a wayside pulpit:

Money will buy a bed but not sleep;
food but not appetite;
finery but not beauty;
a house but not a home;
luxuries but not culture;
amusement but not happiness;
religion but not salvation;
a passport to everywhere – but heaven.

It was once suggested that the Post Office should frank the Christmas mail with an appropriate text from the Bible. One light-hearted sorter suggested that they should put "The Lord Deliver Us".

From Cornwall:

A rather long-winded preacher was dealing with the prophets, one by one. "And where shall I put Isaiah?" he shouted.
A little man in the front row observed, "He can have my seat, I'm going home for my dinner."

Sitting at her desk by the window of her convent, Sister Elizabeth opened a letter from home enclosing a £10 note. Seeing a shabbily-dressed man leaning against a lamp-post in the street below, she quickly wrote "Don't despair – Sister Elizabeth", put it in an envelope with the £10, and dropped it down to the man below.

He nodded, waved thanks and strolled off down the road.

Next day she was told that there was a man at the door asking for her. She found the stranger waiting. Without a word he handed her some money. "What's this?" she asked. "Your winnings, sister, £60. Don't Despair came in at five to one."

CHORAL CHUCKLES

A former chorister was asked why she had given up singing in the church choir. "I was absent one Sunday," she replied, "and somebody asked if the organ had been mended."

The choir was practising the anthem. The choirmaster said to the trebles, "Now don't forget, when the tenors reach 'The Gates of Hell', you come in."

Recently during a morning service the minister announced that the choir would sing 'Far beyond all human comprehension', and they certainly did.

During the practice of the Roger Jones musical *Pharaoh to Freedom* the final song "Man of Sorrows" was not going very well. The choirmaster asked for a repeat starting with: "The guilty, vile and helpless sopranos!"

Member of the congregation to visiting Archdeacon. "And what do you think of our choir?"
"Oh, they were all right," replied the Archdeacon. "Except for that procession in and out, and their singing in between which was dreadful."

An advertisement in Frimley Parish magazine proclaims: "Would you like to see the back of your vicar? Come into the choir stalls and admire the view! Contact the choirmaster."

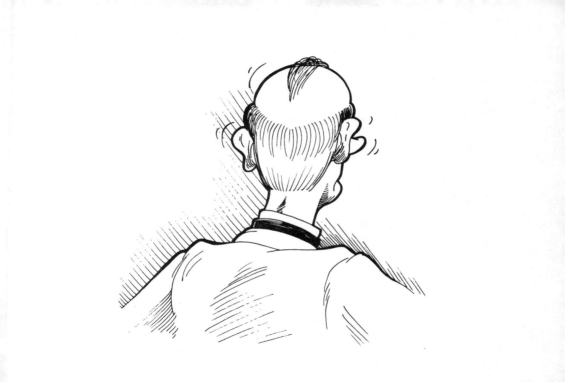

Some years ago when still a schoolboy, I deputised for the organist at a friend's parish church. The parish priest was a blunt Midlander. I slid along the organ bench to say something to one of the men, and the bench suddenly tipped up, and I landed ignominiously on the pedals – with the stops out! A voice from the pulpit thundered: "I let you play your fugues, so kindly let me preach my sermon."

From a Cambridgeshire local paper, circa 1900:

Wanted – a steady respectable able man to look after a garden and milk a cow who has a good voice and is accustomed to singing in a choir.

The choir was in procession down the church when the heel of one of the ladies' shoes got stuck in a metal grating which covered a deep space which at one time had housed the heating system. So as not to cause any confusion the lady slipped her foot out of the shoe and continued walking. The choir member behind her quickly snatched up the shoe but unfortunately the whole grating came up with it. Behind him followed the vicar, still singing as he plunged to the depths below.

At a recent choir practice a definition was sought for the musical term 'syncopation'. The choirmaster defined this as a 'rapid movement between bars'. Some of the choir agreed to try it out after choir practice.

The magazine reported that at a recent choir concert, two members of the choir sang a duet – 'The Lord Knows Why'. Thanks are due to the vicar's wife who laboured all evening on the piano which as usual fell upon her.

A small chapel advertised in the local paper:
Organist required: Small honorarium available.
One reply said "I've never played one, but would not mind trying."

The choir stalls in my church sit below the eye-level of the congregation. Running across the entire front of the church is a low, velvet-draped railing. Several of the more creative choir members discovered that after finishing the anthem they could crawl on hands and knees behind the railing and leave through a side door. They could then buy fresh buns round the corner and return to the morning service undetected.

One Sunday, an elderly, distinguished-looking bass singer made a successful exit. On the return trip, however, he realised that in order to reach his seat, he would have to crawl back carrying the bag of buns between his teeth. It wasn't until he was half-way across that he noticed the laughter spreading throughout the congregation. He was on the wrong side of the railing.

From a Hampshire church magazine:

We badly need more sinners for the choir.